Copyright © 2020 Clavis Publishing Inc., New York

Originally published as *De archeoloog* in Belgium and Holland by Clavis Uitgeverij, Hasselt—Amsterdam, 2010
English translation from the Dutch by Clavis Publishing Inc., New York

Visit us on the Web at www.clavis-publishing.com.

Archaeologists and What They Do written and illustrated by Liesbet Slegers

ISBN 978-1-60537-534-2

This book was printed in April 2020 at Nikara, M. R. Štefánika 858/25, 963 01 Krupina, Slovakia.

First Edition
10 9 8 7 6 5 4 3 2 1

Archaeologists
and What They Do
Liesbet Slegers

Clavis

NEW YORK

It's fun to play dress-up.

But do you ever think about what it was like to live hundreds,
even thousands of years ago?

What kind of clothes did people wear?

What did they eat?

What were their homes like?

How do we learn the answers?

With the help of an archaeologist.

Some things from long ago are still deep in the ground.

A wooden spoon, a piece of a vase, an old coin.

Or perhaps bones from a skeleton or the walls of an old castle.

An archaeologist looks for these kinds of old objects

and digs them up.

Exciting, don't you think?

When an archaeologist is searching for objects,

she wears comfortable clothes.

She has lots of pockets to hold her tools.

Since she works outside, she wears sturdy shoes or boots.

A raincoat comes in handy for bad weather.

She is not worried about getting dirty.

trailer

The archaeologist needs a lot of materials to do her job.

An excavator might dig away the first layer of soil.

Then, a team of archaeologists digs deeper with small tools.

If the archaeologist finds something interesting,

she stores it in a bin or bag.

She measures where the object was found in the ground

and then marks it on a map.

Archaeologists often stay in trailers near the digging site.

excavator

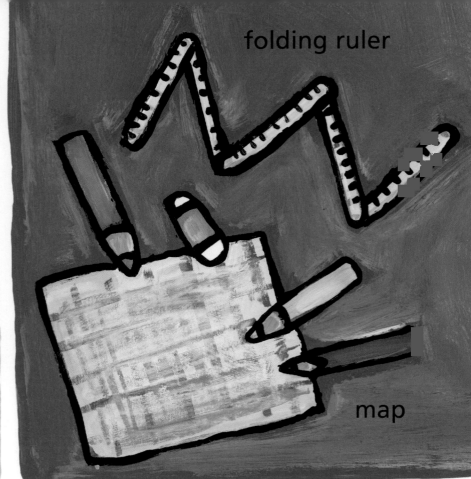

folding ruler

map

bin

bags

dustpan

shovel

trowel

brush

wheelbarrow

An archaeologist's work begins with finding a site to study.

Some sites, such as ancient cities, are visible on the surface.

Other sites are buried deep beneath the ground.

First comes the excavator to shovel away the top layer of soil.

After that, the archaeologists can start to dig with shovels.

The team of archaeologists dig deeper and deeper into the ground.
They work slowly and carefully and keep careful records
of everything that they find.
Sometimes it takes hours, days, or even weeks to make a discovery!

Finally the archaeologist sees something in the soil.

Carefully she scrapes away the ground around it and . . . Look!

She digs some more. Wow, a crown appears!

They take a photograph of the treasure and

mark the location on the map.

The objects that an archaeologist finds are called artifacts.

The artifacts are brushed clean and placed in bins or bags.

They are labeled with information about where they were found.

The archaeologist studies the artifacts and tries
to learn more about them.
Was it the crown of a king? Or of a queen?
What were the coins used for?
The more objects she finds, the more she can learn
about how people used to live.
She uses a computer to research and document her findings.

Archaeologists not only search for artifacts on land.

They may also search in the ocean—for instance in an old boat that

sank long ago. Then they wear diving suits, of course.

Maybe they'll find the skeleton of the ship's captain.

Or pieces of the plates from which the captain ate.

Perhaps there are the remains of an old birdcage?

If you want to see some of these artifacts,

you just have to go to a museum.

There you can learn about the past from the important discoveries

archaeologists have made.

Perhaps you want to become an archaeologist and make

some discoveries of your own?

Buried Treasure

Wouldn't it be fun to bury something in the ground to be discovered later? Maybe an archaeologist will find your treasure one day! Here's what you do:

1 Find an old shoebox or container. Decorate it with crayons or stickers.

2 Gather some objects that will tell someone in the future a little bit about you. Perhaps an old toy. Or a picture you drew. Check with your mom, dad, or a teacher to make sure it's okay to use these items. Write your name and the date on the box.

3 Find a good spot in your yard or in the woods to bury your box. Dig a hole that is big enough for your box.

4 **Put** your treasure box in the hole.

5 **Fill** the hole back up with soil.

6 **Plant** some flowers on top of your treasure if you want. Maybe an archaeologist will find your treasure one hundred years from now . . .